AN EMIGRANT'S WINTER

PUI YING WONG

GLASS LYRE PRESS

ALSO BY PUI YING WONG

POETRY

Mementos

Sonnet for a New Country

Yellow Plum Season

For Tim

And in memory of Damon

*—do not forget
the north wind brings
light from the house of Aries
to the apple trees*

W.G. Sebald

Copyright © 2016 Pui Ying Wong

Paperback ISBN: 978-1-941783-23-8

All rights reserved: except for the purpose of quoting brief passages for review, no part of this book may be reproduced or transmitted in any form or by any means, electronic or mechanical, including photocopying, recording, or by any information storage and retrieval system, without permission in writing from the publisher.

Cover art: "La forêt enchantée" by Christophe Gardner | www.photofrance.fr
Author Photo: Tim Suermondt
Design & layout: Steven Asmussen
Copyediting: Linda E. Kim

Glass Lyre Press, LLC
P.O. Box 2693
Glenview, IL 60026
www.GlassLyrePress.com

Contents

I

The Pink Apartment	13
America is Big	15
See Something Say Something	16
That Kind of Day	17
How Much Heaven	18
On Death and Every Sweet Flying Thing	20
Señora Margarita	22
An Emigrant's Winter	24
Reflection While Waiting for the Laundry, A Quick Study	25
Nan Lian Garden	27
Morning	28
Elegy for the Snow Country	29
Pourquoi Que Je Vis	31
Winter	32

II

Subdivision	35
No Saints in the Neighborhood	37
When the Volcano Erupts	38
Brighton Beach	39
Sunday: Grand Army Plaza	40
November and the Music Box	41
In Sai Kung	42

Small Moments	43
Living the Dream	45
At the Embankment	46
With my Husband in a Little French Town	47
For the Hour	49
Barn Life	50
Mekong	52
In the Shadows of Pagodas	53

III

Every Moment	63
Moan Melody	65
Grass Island	67
Spring, Beijing	69
The Moving Window	71
The Day the Trees Fell	74
The Search	76
At Night When the Air Stirs	77
In Summer's Evening	78
Starlings Over a Town	79
Drizzling in Macau	81
The Algae	82
What I Thought She Meant	83
Risen	84
The Weight of Air	86
Carnival	87
Acknowledgments	89
About the Author	91

I

The Pink Apartment
Sai Kung

It was a low rise building.
The smell of cooked garlic
lingered between the floors,
laughter bursting
from the radios and jokes told
in my native tongue.

I was a stranger at home.
I walked among
the neighbors, quiet
as an unstrung guitar.

I waited for the bus, greeted
by commuters wary like moles
caught in the sun, nothing
could assuage them:
not morning's pure light,
not their own dreams.

I tried to conjure your face
but I was distracted
while you,
like a wayward cloud,
sauntered off.

I listened to rain tapping
on the air conditioner, frogs
silent in the sewer,

my eyes wandering
to the wall where a gecko
mounted itself, playing dead
with its eyes open,

where the paint almost undone
by humidity and time
was blistering
like a tropical illness.

America is Big

Her roads link two oceans,
meeting only in icy water
like her political parties.
Her towns doze in different
time zones like long-
married couples.

Her optimism is gigantic,
we hide our shabby
white flag under the bed.
Her experts speak
like an evangelist
as the world listens.

Her TV channels give us
punchlines and clever chats,
her advertisements
try to sell *you* the real you.

America is big but we can fill her
with our own emptiness.

See Something   Say Something
Sign often seen in New York subway stations

Our bags are heavy,
    so much so a woman sits on hers, exhausted.

She's been lugging batteries,
    bottles of water, masks. Things they say to keep

for emergencies, since one never knows.
    A man opens his suitcase and out flies

a wad of coupons, but redemption is
    nulled by an expiration date.

On the far end of the platform,
    someone reads a collection by Pound. It's 7:15 am

& the poet thought it no more absurd
    than reading the horoscopes

or the financial times. We've already said
    too much, our mouths parched

from repeating the alphabet songs
    as our poems sometimes testify.

A row of fluorescent lights overhead, funereal
    or a white siesta?

The woman gets up with her little boy
    who's quickly a step ahead, hands free.

That Kind of Day

The kind of day that pigeons, flapping

their iron wings, flee. Wind dies.

Rhododendrons' waxy leaves droop

like old men out of breath;

the mailman pushing his cart slowly

like a kabuki actor.

A poet sits at her desk and ponders,

then erases the flickers from the page.

Gray emerges. I bicker. Again,

I don't know the reason for anything.

I press my ear on the pillow

and hear a droning beat, but no music.

Even the dead, tossing in sleep's

brittle husk, refuse to wake.

How Much Heaven

Spring, and the college students
show up like perennials
colonizing the town,
lines at the gas stations,
7-Eleven, cheap Chinese buffets.

I watch the bubble-gum girls,
so much hunger for sun.
So much love for the baby-faced boys,
especially those who thrash out
crass little jokes, trash-talk
their way down to Ft. Lauderdale.

But who can blame them, didn't I
come too, like a battle-wearied ship
looking for blue water, the brightest sky?
If you are like me
waking up every morning
before the birds do,
the day drags on
like the days in childhood,
like the old British Empire
whose sun never set.

You do your best,
make dutiful trips to the post office,
the bank, the pharmacy,
put on a new pair of trousers
for the doctor's appointment.

Even now I ask myself,
waiting here for the early bird special
when the sun has barely left the zenith,
how much light can one tolerate?
How much blue water,
how much heaven?

On Death and Every Sweet Flying Thing

Of course it is absurd to die
by way of a flying banana
that strikes like a brick
at a hundred miles per hour.

Death like this
even in a storm can't compare to,
say, being swept out to sea
or getting knocked off a boulder
which would be heroic
and cause no shame.

And it's not just bananas,
avoid mangoes and pineapples,
avoid every sweet flying thing
coming your way, so
a poet warns.

Who wouldn't want death
for an excruciating old age. If ill,
let it be brief, the mind,
let it be intact, regrets,
let there be none or few.

Think of the woman
daring to spy but getting suffocated
in the chimney of her lover's house,
the man at the stadium

leaping for a foul ball and tumbling
fifty feet below,
or the young cyclist
sent into the oncoming traffic
by a wayward trashcan.

You can argue you have been good
and do not deserve to die
by a fly-by banana, true, but
does your neighbor deserve it more?
The banana, if flying, has
to hit something, right?

Señora Margarita

Do you remember who I am?

You are the one who asks
too many questions.

Have you taken your pills?

I must have. The world is gray.

On a scale of one to ten
what is your pain like?

Like a tree sprouted out of my head,
into heaven—

Your brother in Florida
would love to see you.

Funny, he doesn't dance anymore.

Do you miss church?

God is the one gone missing.

How about the senior center party?

I don't want to dress up
just to meet men with no teeth.

You don't have to.

They say that's the last stop.

An Emigrant's Winter

That winter, water froze in the pipes
and the faucet wheezed like asthma.

Icicles teethed along the power line,
I opened my mouth and my speech stuttered.

The entire city lived in a snow globe,
even big men trod timidly in the wind, hiding their faces
like shamed felons caught by the TV camera.

The market sold out everything,
a young boy snatched the last pack of meat.

Sleet fell all night, tapping
on the windows the way the dead might.

In my dream I went back to the house
that had forgotten about me,
not one there asked how I'd been.

But I sat with them just the same,
watching TV like I had never left.

Who will remember what, who can say?

Mornings punctured by sounds of dragging snowplows,
I peeped at the sun, the feeble white disc,
failed again to burn off the clouds.

It was so cold I could think of fire
and only fire.

Reflection While Waiting for the Laundry, A Quick Study

Cross-legged, almost
catatonic, strange
even to yourself.

Your face placid but
you know it could grimace
like a contortionist's.

Your body disappears
in a black coat,
does it remember

being dressed in
moonshine in a windless cove?
Peace eludes you.

You've accepted that the gate
of enlightenment is for others and
shut that big book of answers.

Instead you seek words
the way a swallow seeks hair,
twigs, for her nest,

your dreams becoming images
springing up like dogs
between parked cars,

soundtracks like the dawn,
a yellow-glow whispering,
the beat of a giant leaving.

Nan Lian Garden
Diamond Hill

Year's end. Musicians perform in the open
and the flutist's notes exile us momentarily
to the land of the dispossessed.
Still green leaves stir in the breeze,
an elder fusses with his high tech camera.
Foreign maids on holiday pose, spreading
their arms like swans. The Gazebo
of Perfection reflects on the pond,
goldenrod in the shadow's folds.
Lotus bursts out too, can a little mud diminish it?
On the height sits Shan Mon, *the mountain gate,*
where the air is chilly but peace awaits,
if only our hearts were purer.
But longing, nemeses of peace, keeps
us at the threshold.
Longing, can we starve it like a beast
till it is no more? The trouble is,
there is no duress in Buddhist poetry,
only sounds of the four winds, snowbirds,
silence of the unclasped hands.
I join the visitors, and start snapping pictures.

Morning

First metaphor some say
has outlasted its use same way
they say about dreams and I suspect
they have not seen how it works itself
in the dark allowing just a hairline split
of itself slowly hacking the horizon
so that it bleeds into the sea like dye
until the sea too is full of life
regardless of what gives the day

Elegy for the Snow Country
Nigata, Japan

That you were never there or even close to it

does not make it less real.

This place in Kawabata's novel,

which you first read in a cheerless room

at an age when you had few memories

and plenty of time,

is both dormant and palpable.

Like places in recurring dreams

this one has accompanied you

through years of lightness and loss,

found you again this February day

in a winter austere as a puritan's love.

Outside the sky is pregnant with clouds.

Snow that has been falling for days still falls.

Your mind drifts like snow

to a landscape of dwarf houses and kerosene lamps,

to Komako the heroine, drunk,

calling out her lover in a voice so pure it burns.

You thought of your first snow

in a city you barely knew, remembering

the sting as you stepped out of the dormitory,

barefoot like a pilgrim might upon a new land

and every molecule in your body screamed live.

Your son's first snow too,

as he watched with astonishment

like a cat catching sight of a spider

climbing in midair,

before language, before naming,

when snow could glisten like clear thought.

What other road if not language

that can take us back to these moments,

to childhood, that first country,

surrounded by savage blue and steep inclines?

What burns cannot be touched but remembered.

What burns in this enigmatic life speeds before you

like a train trundling out of the tunnel

into a valley cold with stars.

Pourquoi Que Je Vis
After Boris Vian

What for do I live then

For the yellow cake
rising like the sun's
pockmarked face
For the insignia
unfurled in a torn sail
For the husks in the tides
calls that go unanswered
For the dark foam
glinting in a tall lager
you drink in a dive bar

pourquoi que je vis
pourquoi que je vis

For the moon
brightening like a hockey rink
when I walk home
after a swim
The day that loses
its zing to sting
For the beachcomber
wading in the sand
wiped clean by the storm

Winter

Flakes drop from your pajamas—

The sky is furry.
Damp air fiddles like rumors
until thick with fidelity.

II

Subdivision

The sun flares behind the silos
   and the neighborhood wakes
in unison.

Automatic coffee pots start
   on time like workers
at government offices.

Showers turn on, full force,
   as if trying to scrub off
the dreams' last trace.

Hydraulic garage doors go up
   without a whine, aligning
themselves with silence.

SUVs roll out of the driveways
   carrying occupants like royals,
or gangsters, in tinted windows.

Sidewalks are swept clean
   as a hospital bed,
after the patient is gone.

Newly planted trees slouch
   like sulky children
getting their hair cut.

In the sunlight, the adjacent farm
    sits vacant, keeping vigil
for missed harvests.

Someone emerges from behind
    the rickety door, and wears
that guilty look of forgetting.

No Saints in the Neighborhood

The silhouette of an oscillating fan appears in one window
like a timid thief keeping look out both ways.
A cat struts on a tall branch, thinking she is still a cougar.
A bronze sun goddess smiles above my neighbor's barbecue pit
till smoke and flames shoot from her mouth on a hot July day.
The pigeon coop next door tilts more each year
and everyone is predicting the time of its demise, since
the owner died and the pigeons no longer come cooing for food.
Satellite dishes have populated the roof and married
the family of chimney pots, broken antennas, trash,
sometimes migratory birds in shock of red or subdued caramel.
At 3am I hear the hissing wind and imagine the Burning Bush.
Where are the Prophets, their premonitions and revelations?
Darkness swallows chairs, keys, shoes in its one-tone dark.
I hear the chaos in my mind like the sound of footsteps ascending
and descending, hovering between the living and the dead.

When the Volcano Erupts

Some say they see it coming.
   Some ask why nobody
warns us. But we
   grab our children,
their stuffed toys, and run.

On the hill a lance of trees
   burn, unstoppable like
someone who bears
   an unbearable grievance,
has set himself on fire.

And we hardly recognize
   the mountain that once gave us
soil so rich, a vista so awe inspiring
   that we burst into praise song, but
now grunts like a pedophile priest.

Ashes rain on our faces
   as we run past the school,
the town hall, the churchyard
   empty. Some say we must
run on our own feet, out of this.

Brighton Beach

Gulls loiter above, a few waddle
on the sand looking for food.

But the summer crowds,
with their tanning oils
and sandcastles, are gone.

The air is at last free of stale beer,
airwaves no longer rocked
by music from box radios.

Even the sea returns to a solemn blue
as if poised to receive kings and pilgrims.

At Café Tatyana, Russian retirees
are having lunch--Borscht and grilled fish.
They eat without hurry, the memory
of breadlines at a safe distance.

Sometimes a man looks up
as if perturbed. He glances toward
the horizon, past a strip of cloud-lit land,
past New Jersey, the Atlantic,
the Bosphorus, the Black Sea

where his youth is,
where the sea is gold at dawn
as he leaps into the waves and swims.

Sunday: Grand Army Plaza

A clown practices silence,
  a mother with a wailing child
waves off the ice cream vendor,
  an elderly man holds a bouquet
in the bend of his arm
  like a newborn.

After a time when every day
  the sky presses down,
long nights when even the streets
  crackle with grief,
we feast on apples, fresh milk,
  like a patient, ravenous after a long illness.

But on the monuments human action
  dies: spears aim only at midair,
half-raised hooves that go nowhere,
  the general's roar expires on his lips.
And in the folds of remembrance's
  black sheen, nothing but blood and tears.

November and the Music Box

The field is ready
for winter,
when it sleeps
it won't get enough

as if something fierce
in the ground is pulling it
down to its core,

then the wind will be homeless
and can't hear its own crackling
in the cornstalks,
the flowering wheat,

and my silence will be
like the music box,
unopened, unwound,
and will grow eyes.

In Sai Kung

I come back to the air of gardenia
and sea brine, where boats rock
like restless children.
The street meanders through villages,
fierce dogs bark at everyone
and at long afternoons.
In the park a huge banyan,
beard flowing like an open dress,
presides over endless card games,
lovers' quarrels and dull rain.

I look for you where the lamppost
was, in the empty prow
of a wobbly wooden boat
like the one we rode,
many summers before,
chatting so idly,
ignorant of the future
as the boatman steered us
away from the shore
where we did similar things,
thought similar thoughts
as other humans did,
like yearning for love,
like being fearful of not living.

Small Moments

Between Joseph Bremen Realty
and San Tay Laundry
someone has roped
his Pomeranian to a sapling,
tied to two skinny poles.

A father helps his little girl
climb a bicycle, nudging
her with encouragement.

In this neighborhood
of Little Leagues and bright lawn chairs,
a day reigns like the one before.

At dawn, the train collects
the commuters like debt,
returning them in the evening
gleaming of sweat.

Noon, young mothers
sip coffee in outdoor cafés,
united by their fidgeting babies,
lack of sleep and
a distraction that has no name.

On the ground of the VA hospital
the gardener with a hose
harbors a spray of rainbow

as if it were a love letter
from the front.

How the day yawns
like a room in need of paint,
silent as a bell missing its clapper.

We ask where time goes,
then fierce barks rend the air,
the sapling has forsaken the streets,
surging skyward.

As for the girl on the bicycle,
she's still training her gaze
on the blurry path,
but no ground
can touch her now.

Living the Dream

Sometimes in the wee hour a dream comes,
giving back what you have lost:

the color of the room in your childhood,
the chug-chug of a train that is forever arriving,
the face of your beloved—
pained and proud,
                      rousing you from stupor.

At the Embankment

December's sharp air in the nostrils,

mist sticky as the anteater's tongue.
Boats clanging on a smorgasbord

of waves, their oars clasped together
like closed wings. Afar,

the island rises like a megafauna,
lights faint in-and-out of the shadows

resembling cat's eye, or pearls
on the nightstand. Nothing is placid

except us, soon to be walking away.

With my Husband in a Little French Town

After dinner we walk up the hill toward the hotel.

The road is narrow and flanked by tall cypresses.

The blackish sky is low with a tinge of blue

emitting from a gas station on the hilltop.

Earlier in the day we got off the train from Paris,

foolishly without a map, every time the road forked

we disagreed which way to go,

then trying to convince the other toward

a direction we ourselves were unsure of.

A bus rolled up and the passengers stared at us.

We must have looked ridiculous in our NY Mets caps,

our bulky backpacks clinging from behind,

in this town smelling of lavender and fresh baked bread.

A taxi drove up but by then we thought

we were almost done with getting lost, with arguing.

What made us think we can parachute into

any place on earth like heroes in the movies?

This morning at *Gare Montparnasse,* you spoke

to the bored clerk in broken English.

You pointed at me and said *"honeymoon!"*

as if that would let him know our destination.

I swore he gave us a look of pity.

You insisted it was envy.

On the train we ate croissants with raspberry jam

and watched the rushing fields, the slow turning turbines.

You said in your dream you had become dyslexic,

you kept on flipping a book backward until I took it away.

Neither of us knew what that meant so we talked

about the places we were going to see,

the chateaus and the vineyards,

the long river flowing through these little towns

that we came to love almost as much as ourselves.

For the Hour

Let there be coffee, eggs
enough for two,
sun to escort the gulls
and students off
to field trips, buttons
on their cardigans
gleaming,

clouds to leave en masse
like tiny islands
liberated from earth,

dragonflies to tilt
their wings, showing off
their unique heliograph,

poplars to fill out like girls
in prom dresses, mysterious
and still growing,

Deliver me from the marsh
of sleep, hissing
dreams of cockroaches
and rubber-tongue lizards, let
my love greet me
at the table, his arms
sprung open like windows.

Barn Life
after Anna Kamienska

At that time sunlight wormed
through the door
apples rotted in the wheelbarrow
cellars reeked of dank earth   motor oil
someone was given dark's little sweet
someone mourned
a clock struck   fender-benders
At that time rifles leaned against the wall
fire roared in the pit   the stew thick
the sound of chains dragged across the floorboard
someone tried to rid a thorn between his teeth
someone shivered someone fanned the fire
coal sparks flew   winter over
At that time air soured of pickled cabbage
sweet with fried dough
it was still a holiday   berries reseeded
someone painted the mountain stream
a little creek   mist in the valley
the moon swelled
someone shouldered a pickaxe
and stumped about in a bear-like gait
At that time trees fell upon trees
peats on the ground spongy
like an old marriage bed
wild turkeys dashed across the yard
someone said a blessing   then the trigger
someone cut open the pig's stomach
and shoved the yams in

At that time everyone ate under the stars
the fire flickered
children danced on the table top
screaming for the clapping to stop

Mekong

Smell of burnt leaves,
a bird shoots up
into the gasoline air,
boats carry pomelo, basil, denim,
buzzing of work, hemlocks sway,
a baby asleep to the blue
of the day, two dogs,
chin down.
How does the river heal?
Crowns of water hyacinth gather
in the river's wide mouth.

In the Shadows of Pagodas

I.
It was winter he loved best:
sand in the wind, the moon
with its icy brightening,
snows orbited swift and wild
as if the gods were testing his resolve.
Who needs the elixir of life
when heaven is waiting?

II.
What made him, Qin Shihuangdi,
who called himself the First Emperor
of China, reigned at the age of thirteen,
conquered seven Warring States,
built Grand Canal in the south,
Great Wall in the north, standardized
currency, measurement and law, then,
ordered all records of historians,
except those of the State of Qin,
be burned; scholars owning
forbidden books, such as the Book of Songs,
be buried alive, answered to no one
but deities whom he prayed to
in the fumigated chamber
clashing of castanets—
turned to his ministers and said *It's time*
that 700,000 men were summoned
to build him his mausoleum?

III.
Machineries of the living world: sunrise,
sunset, tides' ebb and flow, winds' cries
and cessation: a single flower holding
both life and death
and if death must come—
   how bright the hills beckon,
   how lush the valley untainted by decay,
life too shall go on in afterlife
the way stars go on pulsating,
the river flows.
Qinling Mountains in the distance
extended beyond the eyes, the sky bruised
at the horizon, black flags of Qin fluttered
and suddenly it occurred to Qin Sihuangdi
that no sunlight, not a glint
would be let through this tomb mound
soon to be covered by a sweeping green
that was the gateway to the underworld.
For there's a limit to symmetry
even for an emperor,
in reconstructing the cosmos.

IV.
Without armies there would be no empire—
generals, warriors, archers,
bowmen, infantrymen,
even if they were made of clay.
Figures varied in size, poise,
painted in resin, lacquer,
their color bright,
their faces individual
as if each were bestowed a spirit,
each could breathe, could kill.
Near them were sculpted horses, chariots,
real weapons like spears, swords and shields,
crossbows, gold coins, bells, jades
in heaps, pit to pit
below one celestial sky
where a hundred mercury rivers flowed,
a thousand dugong oil-lit flames
flamed. Who says anything is ephemeral?

V.
The chosen were just that, chosen for.
Their fate sealed, be they the counselors,
musicians, acrobats, concubines
who had borne no sons would accompany
the Emperor to the afterlife.
When the gate of the mausoleum
shut behind them, did they
cling together like bees to nectar,
cry the kind of cry only the gods
could bear hearing?
In life no one was not his subject,
and in death?
The emperor buried in the grave
was unapproachable in death
as he was in life, but he, too,
was the chosen. The son of Heaven,
filial, ritualistic, upholding pattern
that was the universe, replica
to replica, true heir
to the illusory life.

VI.
In the water garden for the afterlife
lilies rose and bloomed.
If the main tomb bears the emblem
of order and power,
Qin Shihuangdi, the heaven anointed,
sole ruler of right and wrong,
giver of reward and punishment,
must not abdicate his duties.
But the mind too must rest,
must properly prepare for the next
and, yes, the celestial being
whom he strived to be
dwelled only in the over-world—
seen from there, afterlife
was just a dream.
Away from the everyday necropolis
he would seek respite in the water garden
among bronze geese and swans,
where lilies borne of muck
would not succumb to muck.

VII.
In the shadows of pagodas
he contemplated, beauties sang
unfailingly under the willow.
A world wedded to death but no
dying, a world without light or air,
and water never changing course,
ran through brooks, bog to bog,
dream upon dream.

III

Every Moment

This afternoon unable to write
I watch numbing white lights
in the yard cut in
by a descending cardinal
flapping its scarlet wings
like a wind-up toy.
The intensity of the bird's color
jolts me and suddenly I remember
the story by Tennessee Williams
I read long ago. The heroine
in Oriflamme woke up one morning,
found the air cleansed after
a long sullen season.
I hurt as Anna examined her naked body,
shrunk in the days of dull.
Her skin bore the color of chalk.
Blue veins flowered.
I cheered as Anna fought the store clerks
(busily dispensing the don'ts)
for the red silk dress, ablaze
in the front window—her battle flag
to the anarchy of drab.
Is it true that a grain of renewal
is buried in every moment? Here I am
in a day sprayed and scrubbed.

Anything can happen now.
Wars ended or declared,
an expedition begun.
Bird, can you stand sentry for a while.
Show me how to untwist the flame.

Moan Melody

"But I spin all these crazy yarns
as if sleeping in a mound of narrative"
—Zbigniew Herbert—

Maze of market streets,
bric-a-brac, flowers, shoes,
browsers' faces, gazes

that peel night to day,
little cars going around
in search of
ascend, descend, yield---

to who, to whom
these red lights blink and blink,
crosswalks, guardrails,
scurf pegged air, there's heart
in what you keep opening to,

a man leans on the horn
as if he's waited
his whole life, enough,
how else can we get through
and get to, please,

the station master speaks,
just another foreign tongue
but the gesture is clear,
no tickets, the phone,

what is your number, dear,
write it down, your number,
the number must reach.

Grass Island

December, it's cold, but the visitors
keep their spirits, looking for a souvenir
like pilgrims searching for a new life,
though it's just key chains,
magnets, hats.

In food stalls, shrimps shed grey
for gold, a transformation
that also shrinks them.
Cuttlefish lose their antennas,
crabs get to keep their claws,
strung up like someone
with too many doctrines.

In a restaurant, city workers on holiday
converse about workplaces,
the injustice they suffer,
the revenge they would like to take.
Hard to tell if they've just arrived
or are waiting for the next ferry.
The maître d', having heard it all, brings out
the dishes, serenely as a sexton
who's just rung the day's last bells.

But we know the island is no cathedral,
there are no flying buttresses
or a soaring choir stunning us
to believe, if for an instant, we are
the rightful heirs, our prayers true.

All that remain are
the salt in the air,
lulling waves,
and a fisherman in a stained shirt,
counting up what the year is worth.

Spring, Beijing

Boulevards wide as airfields,
the vast square meant
for armies and chariots
is crowded with hawkers.

A guard stands in attention
at the crossing, expressionless
as the five red stars
pinned on his lapel.

Flag poles have been planted
firmly along the moat,
and the warning signs read:
Fishing Strictly Forbidden.

Poplars everywhere,
slender like the young women
strolling arm in arm with their
parasols, leaving trails of laughter
and shells of sunflower seeds.

In the park a crowd gathers,
alert as an alley cat.
A man sings falsetto.
We don't know the lyrics
but we hear a music that lives
between timidity
and bravery.

Bicycles are disappearing fast
along with the *hutongs*
where tourists in courtyard inns
trade tips on currency exchange
and roasted-duck restaurants.

By the foundation site
across the long gray wall,
a migrant worker emerges
from under a sheet of plastic,
a makeshift tent
for his cot and portable TV.

He looks into the morning
that is fish-belly white,
catkins swirling in the air
as if they have just been
blown out of his dream.

The Moving Window

1. Postcard From Winter

Snow dulls me,
too much, too long.

It caves like a heart
drained of desire.

In the center is a key. But
it is bent and won't open any door.

2. From the Hotel Window

A crow nosedives
from the rooftop, swoops up
and does it again.

Why when it could fly straight,
be as single-minded
as an ideologue.

3. At the Golden-Gate Bridge Bus Stop

The driver yells at the tourists.
"Step up! We got places to go."

Maybe he is one of us:
restless when rested,

a faithful lover of a moving window.

4.   *Chinese Couplet*

My agitated heart tells me I am alive.

When peace comes I listen to the four winds.

*   *   *

Ancient poets look east and think of spring,
look west and think of autumn.

To my east there is memory,
to my west there is time,
unbridled time beyond which
it should not be my business.

5.   *In Bed Hearing Rain Come*

Battalions of arrows, fired by whose
  archers from what other world?

6.   *What Joy Can Be*

To be with your beloved in a town
  so small it's off the map,
to be ignorant of its language and its wars.

To fix your gaze on its whisky-colored sunset,
to not remembering you have a past and a future.

7.   *Late Dance*

Memory returns to salvage what it can.
Time trots ahead as if tired of being riffled through.

8.   *The Vanishing City*

They can rename the streets, the monuments,
the schools, the parks—
they existed in your city
and will vanish only with you.

The Day the Trees Fell

Did it matter
if they were mulberry
or elm, gingko
or oak

did it matter
if they started to leaf
or rust, stood apart
or leaned together
like lovers

unkempt or pruned
to perfection,
did it matter

if we planted them
for shade
as buffer
in the front lawn

if we dressed them
in tinsel, fake snow,
in strings of lights
awaiting gods or angels

twined tiny tubes
around their limbs

fed them water
in drought year

if their thuds would have
wakened Hades, the musty smell
of their upturned roots
was the underground,

the sacrilegious air.

The Search

Even long after the rescue
has been called off, we rouse
in the middle of the night
and head out the door, our blankets,
flashlights in hand,
and stumble down the back porch's
icy steps, hearing behind us
the screen door shutting.

Moonlight falls like a bolt
of silk. On the moon's face
the blotches are the ones
we see all our lives.
No longer do we believe
in the moon goddess
who night after night
mixes potions to make us
well. What good is her benevolence
if it won't return the ones we lost?

The dog stays by our side,
barks every now and then
as if to calm his fear.
We come upon the same path,
the one we believe will lead us
to a clue if not the answer. But again,
tonight, the thickets yield nothing.
Then the towering trees,
resolute as the coming dark, closing in.

At Night When the Air Stirs

The war is in the distance
    but coffins arrive at night by plane
as we sleep in our house and the pipes
    are the only things that weep.

When Salvator Giunta was awarded
    the Medal of Honor he spoke
of his dead buddies and the night
    when the sky had more bullets than stars.

I had marched against the war
    and heard my own voice soar and dip
and slip like a fish back to the sea.

In a city called Hom the dictator's bombs
    drop on his people and a survivor
lashes out at the TV cameras, asking
    why do you watch us die?

In the quiet of my house I look out
    and see neither bullets nor stars
I watch and watch, my tongue tied.

In Summer's Evening

Friends gather in a jasmine-
scented garden, drink
wine from Sonoma and listen
to tales of travel: Tuscany,
Chartres, an ashram in India.

Then someone says the President
is a war criminal, and no one
contradicts. The talk turns
to the number of dead, the cost,
whom the war serves. At last,

sounds of leaves rustling take over,
we say goodbye, returning
home, returning to the wars
which lurk in ourselves
    in insomnia,
        in the purge hours.

Starlings Over a Town
In Kentucky

No one knows why they come but here
they congregate, in shiny black suits
like politicians who have arrived with a plan.
In the midst of winter quiet, more suitable
for contemplation or conducting illicit affairs,
residents hear instead the clashing of wings,
sudden bursts of shrieks as if the seams
of calm days have finally come off.
Neighbors chat up what they observe:
do some flocks favor the grand roof
of the library where the sages live
undisturbed on the shelves,
or above the bus terminal, hotspot
for mosquitoes and men with time?
Even the homebound are curious,
peering through heavy curtains
at a scene they don't recognize.
Newsmen come with cameras,
theories and anecdotes,
an ornithologist is interviewed
on TV, more experts speak.
Someone mentions Hitchcock, Bodega Bay,
the blond actress in a smart yellow dress.
How everything relates to everything!
Winter lingers. The starlings nest.
Soon, some admit sights of bird droppings
on their windshields, driveways,
make them feel singled out.

The dogs whine.
The mayor chimes in.
Residents form a squad, a timetable is set.
As the first waves of pots and pans
thunder, an ensemble of birds fly away
like a good guest, or a bowing magician
toward the finishing act,
tossing in the sky his smoky black cape.

Drizzling in Macau

The evening damp
as a bat's cave,
the Ruin of St. Paul's dissolves
in the dark, the priest
takes a holiday.
Idle vendors pace,
a round of gin rummy slouches
in a dingy storefront. Mists
descend from the South China Sea,
salty as shrimp paste.
Pedicabs race down the hill.
Casino lights explode in the fog.
Fleets of limousines await
as if the mob boss's funeral
has finally happened.
Another ferry arrives. A man
with an assured look,
like someone who never believes
he could lose it all, hops off.

The Algae

We were driving around,
along the main road
then across the canal.
The air had been stale
for days, for months,
no relief, no rain in the forecast.

All through the neighborhood
barbers gave the same haircut,
preachers gave the same sermon,
busy people pressed on with the heart
of a mule. Had it been that long
since childhood eloped?

And poetry languishing,
curled up in a musty folder.
Without poetry—would our lives
(Could we fool ourselves
anymore) go on as before?

Only the algae bloomed.
Only the algae bloomed.

What I Thought She Meant

My cat died last night.

At first her breathing grew weaker,

her tail throbbed and then stopped.

I lifted her paw. There was no resistance

and sixteen years of our lives

blinked in that instant.

Her eyes were still open, glassy.

Forget me now. Forget me.

Risen

A cake has risen in the oven,
golden as Van Gogh's sunflowers,
a poor girl's match light,
moonbeams in the black dog's eyes.

So much has been taken from you: love,
dreams, time. When strangers ask,
like the psychiatrist needs case histories,
the usher needs tickets,
Doubting Thomas needed the wound,
you refuse to answer.

Do they know they cannot hold still the clouds,
handcuff the thunder?

Do they know memory is not the wax replica
in the museum, but is infused with love,
dreams, time?

You are left with papers, words, some foreign.
You write about dawn that is the dawn.
Silver taxis move in the night like minnows,
the way your beloved once walked toward you
and could not be mistaken for anything
but joy.

Moonbeams in the black dog's eyes.
A poor girl's match light,
golden as Van Gogh's sunflowers.
A cake has risen in the oven.

The Weight of Air

The streets in this town hug
the neighborhood in a curl.
Brownstones tout their heavy past,
stained glass, candelabra,
gas lamps glow in a swirl of dust.
Morning washes the flagstones white.
Black birds flit to and fro,
shadow into light, light into shadow.
Memories untangled from time's thicket.
I've exhausted even speech, even speech.
Might every poem be a prayer,
a horse's neigh upon a precipice?
I've wedded to this earth, to its fruits
to its perils, I've held on
like an air root, like an air root.

Carnival

Everyone walks on air,

swallows fog

out of which cities rose,

gold domes, gray spires, grazing

at clouds, at lost signals:

rooms of convex mirrors

rooms stuffed with flowers

rooms stalked of deep shadows,

long goodbyes.

Always one more road,

one more character, a clown and his

pantomime, a refugee woman

sewn to her shawl, a heartbreaker, nod

as if they know me. Even I smile

back to this world, at me.

Acknowledgments

I would like to thank my family and friends for their support and inspiration, especially to poets Lee Slonimsky and Gloria Mindock.

Grateful acknowledgement is also made to the editors of the publications in which the following poems first appeared:

decomP: "An Emigrant's Winter"

Prairie Schooner: "Brighton Beach," "Grass Island"

The Southampton Review: "When the Volcano Erupts," "Sunday: Grand Army Plaza"

Pirene's Fountain: "For the Hour," "The Weight of Air," "In Summer's Evening"

Connotation Press: An Online Artifact: "Nan Lian Garden"

2Bridges Review: "Drizzling in Macau"

Valparaiso Poetry Review: "Spring, Beijing"

Red River Review: "The Day the Trees Fell"

Blood Lotus Journal: "How Much Heaven"

Ucity Review: "No Saints in the Neighborhood," "Carnival"

The Brooklyner: "With My Husband in a Little French Town"

Brooklyn Voice: "Every Moment"

Gargoyle: "That Kind of Day"

Foundling Review: "At Night When the Air Stirs"

The New Poet:	"In Sai Kung"
The Boiler Journal:	"November and the Music Box," "Mekong"
Literary Bohemian:	"The Pink Apartment"
A Narrow Fellow:	"What I Thought She Meant," "Small Moments"
Angle Poetry:	"Elegy for the Snow Country," "Starlings over a Town"
Offcourse:	"Barn Life," "At the Embankment," "Morning," "Living the Dream"
Gravel:	"Pourquoi Que Je Vis," "The Moving Window," "See Something Say Something"
Slippery Elm:	"Risen," "On Death & Every Sweet Flying Thing"
Taos Journal of Poetry & Art	"Subdivision," "The Search"
Cha: An Asian Literary Journal:	"In the Shadows of Pagodas"
Cosmonauts Avenue:	"Winter"
Mojave River Review:	"Moan Melody," "The Algae"
Bagelbard Anthology:	"Reflection While Waiting for the Laundry, a Quick Study"

About the Author

Pui Ying Wong was born in Hong Kong. She is the author of a full-length book of poetry *Yellow Plum Season* (New York Quarterly Books, 2010), two chapbooks: *Mementos* (Finishing Line Press, 2007), *Sonnet for a New Country* (Pudding House Press, 2008). She has poems in *Prairie Schooner, The Southampton Review, Plume Poetry Journal, The New York Times, decomP, The Brooklyner* and *Pirene's Fountain,* among others. She is a book reviewer for Cervena Barva Press in Somerville. She lives in Cambridge (MA) with her husband, the poet Tim Suermondt.

Glass Lyre Press

exceptional works to replenish the spirit

Glass Lyre Press is an independent literary publisher interested in technically accomplished, stylistically distinct, and original work. Glass Lyre seeks diverse writers that possess a dynamic aesthetic and an ability to emotionally and intellectually engage a wide audience of readers.

Glass Lyre's vision is to connect the world through language and art. We hope to expand the scope of poetry and short fiction for the general reader through exceptionally well-written books, which evoke emotion, provide insight, and resonate with the human spirit.

Poetry Collections
Poetry Chapbooks
Select Short & Flash Fiction
Anthologies

www.GlassLyrePress.com

www.ingramcontent.com/pod-product-compliance
Lightning Source LLC
Chambersburg PA
CBHW021157080526
44588CB00008B/382